Helen Steiner Rice

A

Book

of

Hope

Compiled by Virginia J. Ruehlmann

Fleming H. Revell
A Division of Baker Book House
Grand Rapids, Michigan 49516

Published by Fleming H. Revell
a division of Baker Book House Company
P.O. Box 6287, Grand Rapids, MI 49516-6287

Third printing, May 1998

Printed in the United States of America

ISBN 0-8007-1722-8

Jacket and interior illustrations by Jack Brouwer

Scripture selections marked NAB are from the *New American Bible* © 1991, 1986, 1970
Confraternity of Christian Doctrine, Washington, D.C. Used with permission.

Scripture quotations marked NIV are from the HOLY BIBLE, NEW
INTERNATIONAL VERSION®. NIV®. Copyright © 1973, 1978, 1984 by
International Bible Society. Used by permission of Zondervan Publishing House. All
rights reserved.

Scripture quotations marked RSV are from the Revised Standard Version of the Bible,
copyright 1946, 1952, 1971, and 1973 by the Division of Christian Education of the
National Council of the Churches of Christ in the United States of America.

For current information about all releases from Baker Book House, visit our web
site:

http://www.bakerbooks.com/

To: _Lottie_ ~~from~~ with love

From: _Luster_

When you're troubled and worried and sick at heart
And your plans are upset, and your world falls apart,
Remember God's ready and willing to share
The burden you find much too heavy to bear.
So with hope, "let go" and "let God" lead the way
Into a brighter and less troubled day —
For God has a plan for everyone
If we learn to pray, "Thy will be done."

THE HELEN STEINER RICE FOUNDATION

When someone does a kindness
It always seems to me
That's the way God up in heaven
Would like us all to be . . .

Whatever the celebration, whatever the day, whatever the event, whatever the occasion, Helen Steiner Rice possessed the ability to express the appropriate feeling for that particular moment in time. Her positive attitude, her concern for others, and her love of God are identifiable threads woven into her life, her work . . . and even her death.

Prior to Mrs. Rice's passing, she established the HELEN STEINER RICE FOUNDATION, a non-profit corporation that awards grants to worthy charitable programs assisting the elderly and the needy.

Royalties from the sale of this book will add to the financial capabilities of the HELEN STEINER RICE FOUNDATION. Because of limited resources, the foundation presently limits grants to qualified charitable programs in Lorain, Ohio, where Helen Steiner Rice was born and Greater Cincinnati, Ohio, where Mrs. Rice lived and worked most of her life. Hopefully in the future resources will be of sufficient size that broader areas may be considered in the awarding of grants. Thank you for your assistance in helping to keep Helen's dream alive and growing.

Andrea R. Cornett, Administrator

Dedicated
to those individuals
who are
in search of hope
and to those
who are
sustained by hope
when facing challenging situations
and who, by example,
inspire hope
in others

Contents

Hope for Tomorrow

How often we wish for another chance
  to make a fresh beginning—
A chance to blot out our mistakes
  and change failure into winning.
And it does not take a new day
  to make a brand-new start,
It only takes a deep desire
  to try with all our heart
To live a little better
  and to always be forgiving
And to add a little sunshine
  to the world in which we're living.
So never give up in despair
  And think that you are through,
For there's always a tomorrow
  and the hope of starting new.

Introduction

Hope springs eternal in the human breast.
Ancient maxim

Hope is the virtue by which we trust and maintain a confidence in God's promises. Hope is closely interwoven with faith and charity.

Hope gives promise of a future blessing. To possess hope is to have confidence and to maintain a trust. It is that inherent quality which sustains an individual while patiently anticipating a favorable outcome.

Helen Steiner Rice lived a life filled with optimism. She learned and passed along to others the merit of maintaining a positive attitude. Many of her poems convey the value of remaining hopeful, rather than becoming discouraged, depressed, or downhearted.

One of her favorite sayings was "Let go and let God!" This expression puts into capsulated form the directions for increasing hope in one's life.

May this collection of Helen's poems serve as a road map to guide you on your journey of a lifetime filled with hope.

Hopefully,
Virginia J. Ruehlmann

The art of
 foreseeing a positive outcome,
 expecting the dream we dream to come true,
 feeling that we can and will achieve our goals —
these are indeed aspects of hope.

Hope, they say, deserts us at no period of our existence. From first to last, and in the face of smarting disillusions, we continue to expect good fortune, better health and better conduct, and that so confidently that we judge it needless to deserve them.

Robert Louis Stevenson

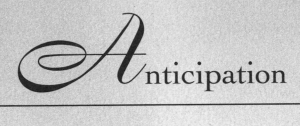

Anticipation

*E*ven if our today is filled with sadness and defeat, who can foretell what the next day will bring to us? Let us all eagerly await what destiny will deal us. We speak of man meeting his fate, and we speak truthfully, for every day we see life converged to life.

Tomorrow may hold your fate; tomorrow may mean your victory. The great joy of expectation, the wonderment of an unknown realm, the splendor of the vast, unlimitable future all lie in the eternal tomorrow—the day which makes life worth living.

H.S.R.

I Come to Meet You

I come to meet You, God, and as I linger here
I seem to feel you're very near.
A rustling leaf, a rolling slope
Speak to my heart of endless hope.
The sun just rising in the sky,
The waking birdlings as they fly,
The grass all wet with morning dew
Are telling me I just met You.
And, gently, thus the day is born
As night gives way to breaking morn,
And once again I've met You, God,
And worshipped on Your holy sod—
For who could see the dawn break through
Without a glimpse of heaven and You?
For who but God could make the day
And softly put the night away?

You answer us with awesome deeds of righteousness, O God our Savior, the hope of all the ends of the earth and of the farthest seas.
                                                    Psalm 65:5 NIV

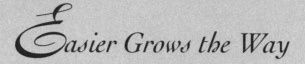

Easier Grows the Way

Looking ahead, the hills seem steep
  and the road rises up to the sky,
But as we near them and start to climb,
  they never seem half as high.
And thinking of work and trouble,
  we worry and hesitate,
But just as soon as we tackle the job,
  the burden becomes less great.
So never a hill, a task or load,
  a minute, an hour, a day,
But as we grow near it and start to climb,
  easier grows the way.

After Each Storm of Life

The rainbow is God's promise
of hope for you and me,
And though the clouds hang heavy
and the sun we cannot see,
We know above the dark clouds
that fill the stormy sky
Hope's rainbow will come shining through
when the clouds have drifted by.

There are no rules of architecture for a castle in the clouds.
Gilbert Keith Chesterton

The Seasons of the Soul

Why am I cast down and despondently sad
When I long to be happy and joyous and glad?
I ask myself often what makes life this way —
Why is the song silenced in the heart today?
And then with God's help it all becomes clear —
The soul has its seasons just the same as the year.
I too must pass through life's autumn of dying,
A desolate period of heart-hurt and crying,
Followed by winter, in whose frostbitten hand
My heart is as frozen as the snow-covered land.

Yes, man too must pass through the seasons God sends,
Content in the knowledge that everything ends . . .
And oh, what a blessing to know there are reasons
And to find that the soul too must have its seasons —
Bounteous seasons and barren ones too,
Times for rejoicing and times to be blue —
And to meet these seasons of dark desolation
With strength that is born of anticipation
That comes from knowing that autumntime sadness
Will surely be followed by a springtime of gladness.

Hope is outreaching desire with expectancy of good.
Edward S. Ames

Remembrance Road

There's a road I call remembrance
  where I walk each day with you.
It's a pleasant, happy road,
  all filled with memories true.
Today it leads me through a spot
  where I can dream awhile,
And in its tranquil peacefulness
  I touch your hand and smile.

There are hills and fields and budding trees
  and stillness that's so sweet,
It seems that this must be the place
  where God and humans meet.
I hope we can go back again
  and golden hours renew,
And God go with you always,
  until the day we do.

Today's Joy

Who said the darkness of the night
   would never turn to day?
Who said the winter's bleakness
   would never pass away?
Why should we ever entertain
   these thoughts so dark and grim
And let the brightness of our minds
   grow cynical and dim,
When we know beyond all questioning
   that winter turns to spring
And on the notes of sorrow
   new songs are made to sing?
No one sheds a teardrop
   or suffers loss in vain,
For God is always there to turn
   our losses into gain . . .
And every burden borne today
   and every present sorrow
Are but God's happy harbingers
   of a joyous, bright tomorrow.

There is no medicine like hope, no incentive so great, and no tonic so powerful as expectation of something tomorrow.

Orison Swett Marden

Put Your Soul in God's Control

Many trials and troubles
   are scattered on our way—
Daily little crosses
   are a part of every day.
But the troubles we have suffered
   are over, past, and through,
So why should bygone happenings
   keep gravely troubling you?
The problems that beset us
   in the now and present hour
We need not try to solve alone
   without God's grace and power,
And those scheduled for tomorrow
   still belong to God alone—
They are still unborn and formless
   and a part of the unknown.

So let us face the trouble
    that is ours this present minute
And count on God to help us
    and to put His mercy in it,
And forget the past and future
    and dwell wholly on today,
For God controls the future
    and He will direct our way.

We do not need more intellectual power, we need more spiritual power . . . We do not need more of the things that are seen, we need more of the things that are unseen.

Calvin Coolidge

The ability to
address the challenges before you with a brave mind,
embrace a positive attitude as you face all obstacles,
believe that an inner strength resides within you —
these are indeed aspects of hope.

Therefore, since we have been justified through faith, we have peace with God through our Lord Jesus Christ, through whom we have gained access by faith into this grace in which we now stand. And we rejoice in the hope of the glory of God.

Romans 5:1–2 NIV

Courage

I just want to say again that if we never suffered tragedy and we never felt sorrow, how could our souls grow? In my husband's tragic death, which was so hurried and unscheduled, it was difficult for me, when I was very young, to see what the purpose could have been. But now I know that he sacrificed his life that my life might be lived in a fuller and richer way, for his sudden death transformed my entire life. I could never have done what I am doing now if I had not felt the pangs of sorrow, for you cannot dry the tears of those who weep unless you have cried yourself.

H.S.R.

What Will You Do with This Day?

As we start a new day, untouched and unmarred,
Unblemished and flawless, unscratched and unscarred,
May we try to do better and accomplish much more
And be kinder and wiser than in the day gone before.
Let us wipe our slate clean and start over again,
For God gives this privilege to sincere women and men
Who will humbly admit they have failed many ways
But are willing to try and improve their new days
By asking God's help in all that they do
And counting on Him to refresh and renew
Their courage and faith when things go wrong
And the way seems dark and the road rough and long.
What will you do with this day that's so new?
The choice is yours—God leaves that to you!

If you have built castles in the air, your work need not be lost; that is where they should be. Now put foundations under them.

Henry David Thoreau

This Too Will Pass Away

If I can endure for this minute
    whatever is happening to me,
No matter how heavy my heart is
    or how dark the moment might be—
If I can remain calm and quiet
    with all my world crashing about me,
Secure in the knowledge God loves me
    when everyone else seems to doubt me—
If I can but keep on believing
    what I know in my heart to be true,
That darkness will fade with the morning
    and that this will pass away too—
Then nothing in life can defeat me,
    for as long as this knowledge remains,

I can suffer whatever is happening,
    for I know God will break all the chains
That are binding me tight in the darkness
    and trying to fill me with fear,
For there is no night without dawning,
    and I know that my morning is near.

*Faith is to believe what we do not see; and the reward of this faith
is to see what we believe.*

                                Saint Augustine

Comparison

We wouldn't enjoy the sunshine
   if we never had the rain.
We wouldn't appreciate good health
   if we never experienced pain.
If we never shed a teardrop
   and always wore a smile,
We'd all get tired of laughing
   after we had grinned awhile.
Everything is by comparison—
   both the bitter and the sweet—
And it takes a bit of both of them
   to make our lives complete.

Why are you downcast, O my soul? Why do you sigh within me?
Hope in God! For I shall again be thanking him, in the presence
of my savior and my God.

Psalm 42:6 NAB

When Hope Is High

No burden is too heavy,
   no way is too long
If your hope is high
   and your faith is strong.

For thou, O Lord, art my hope, my trust, O LORD, from my youth.
Psalm 71:5 RSV

You Too Must Weep

Let me not live a life that's free
From the things that draw me close to Thee,
For how can I ever hope to heal
The wounds of others I do not feel?
If my eyes are dry and I never weep,
How do I know when the hurt is deep?
If my heart is cold and it never bleeds,
How can I tell what my brother needs?
For when ears are deaf to the beggar's plea
And we close our eyes and refuse to see
And we steel our hearts and harden our minds
And we count it a weakness whenever we're kind,
We are no longer following the Father's way
Or seeking His guidance from day to day.
So spare me no heartache or sorrow, dear Lord,
For the heart that hurts reaps the richest reward,
And God blesses the heart that is broken with sorrow
As He opens the door to a brighter tomorrow —
For only through tears can we recognize
The suffering that lies in another's eyes.

For through the Spirit, by faith, we wait for the hope of righteousness.
Galatians 5:5 RSV

A Message of Consolation

On the wings of death and sorrow
God sends us new hope for tomorrow,
And in His mercy and His grace,
He gives us strength to bravely face
The lonely days that stretch ahead
And knowledge our loved one is not dead
But only sleeping out of our sight,
And we'll meet in the land
Where there is no night.

Therefore my heart is glad and my tongue rejoices; my body also will live in hope, because you will not abandon me to the grave, nor will you let your Holy One decay.

Acts 2:26–27 NIV

Words of Truth

In this ever-changing world
   God's words remain unchanged,
Although through countless ages
   they've been often rearranged,
And the words of inspiration
   that I write for you today
Are just the old enduring truths
   said in a rhythmic way.
And if my borrowed words of truth
   in some way touch your heart,
Then I am deeply thankful
   to have had a little part
In sharing these God-given lines,
   so simple and so true,
And may you, in turn, share them
   with friends and loved ones too.

The LORD delights in those who fear him, who put their hope in his unfailing love.

Psalm 147:11 NIV

Trouble Is a Steppingstone to Growth

Trouble is something no one can escape—
Everyone has it in some form or shape.
Some people hide it way down deep inside,
Some people bear it with gallant-like pride.
Some people worry and complain of their lot,
Some people covet what they haven't got
While others rebel and become bitter and old
With hopes that are dead and hearts that are cold.
But the wise man accepts whatever God sends,
Willing to yield like a storm-tossed tree bends,
Knowing that God never makes a mistake,
So whatever God sends he is willing to take.
For trouble is part and parcel of life,
And no man can grow without struggle or strife,
And the steep hills ahead and the high mountain peaks
Afford man at last the peace that he seeks.

So blessed are the people who learn to accept
The trouble men try to escape and reject,
For in our acceptance we're given great grace
And courage and faith and the strength to face
The daily troubles that come to us all,
So we may learn to stand straight and tall—
For the grandeur of life is born of defeat,
For in overcoming we make life complete.

Trouble is like a stone wall that cannot be moved by worry or wishing; nor will it be moved by self-pity. The only tools that will wear away the stones are faith, hope, cheerfulness, and perseverance, used in the hands of an undaunted toiler.

Lucille R. Taylor

My Prayer

Whenever I'm discouraged
    and lost in deep despair,
I bundle all my troubles up
    and go to God in prayer.
But there are many, many times
    He seems so far away
That I can't help but wonder
    if He hears me when I pray.
Then I beseech Him earnestly
    to hear my humble plea,

To tell me how to serve Him
and to do it gallantly.
And so I pray this little prayer
and hope that He will show me
How I can bring more happiness
to all the folks who know me —
To give me hope and courage,
enough for every day,
And faith to light the darkness
when I stumble on my way,
And love and understanding,
enough to make me kind,
So I may judge all people
with my heart and not my mind.

What would this world be without hope? It is the light in the darkness, joy in sorrow, and strength in weakness; without it the world would be desolate indeed. Its beams are like a great searchlight shining in our hearts, and brightening up every corner, until we mount, as with wings, over difficulties and circumstances, and triumph glorious over the enemy, despair.

Ida Scott Taylor

The supernatural gift to
  believe in God, Our Creator, and all that He has revealed,
  trust in the evidence of things not visible to the eye,
  recognize that miracles do happen —
these are indeed aspects of hope.

To us also, through every star, through every blade of grass, is not God made visible if we will open our minds and our eyes?

Thomas Carlyle

Faith

*M*y outlook on life is just the simple outlook that faith provides for each one of
us if we do not attempt to remake God
into a God of our own specifications, who meets our own
selfish needs. I am a very simple, uncomplicated person,
and a child's faith is all I possess.

I try to brighten the corner wherever I happen to be.
Knowing that life is forever and nothing is ever by chance
or happenstance but by divine design, I accept whatever
happens, be it pleasure or pain, as a gift from God. View-
ing it that way makes everything understandable.

H.S.R.

Great Faith Is Born of Trials

It's easy to say "In God we trust"
  when life is radiant and fair,
But the test of faith is only found
  when there are burdens to bear.
For our claim to faith in the sunshine
  is really no faith at all,
For when roads are smooth and days are bright
  our need for God seems so small.
And no one discovers the fullness
  or the greatness of God's love
Unless they have walked in the darkness
  with only a light from above.
For the faith to endure whatever comes
  is born of sorrow and trials
And strengthened only by discipline
  and nurtured by self-denials.
So be not disheartened by troubles,
  for trials are building blocks
On which to erect a fortress of faith,
  secure on God's ageless rocks.

Honor begets honor; trust begets trust; faith begets faith; and hope is the mainspring of life.

Henry L. Stimson

The Hope of the World

An empty tomb, a stone rolled away
Speak of the Savior who rose Easter Day,
But that was centuries and centuries ago
And we ask today — Was it really so?
We were not there to hear or see,
But our hopes and dreams of eternity
Are centered around the Easter story
When Christ ascended and rose in glory.
For after the Lord was crucified,
Even the ones who had scoffed and denied
Knew that something had taken place
That nothing could ever remove or erase.
For hope was born in the soul of man,
And faith to believe in God's master plan
Stirred in the hearts to dispel doubt and fear,
And that faith has grown with each passing year.
For the hope of man is the Easter story,
And life is robbed of all meaning and glory
Unless man knows that he has a goal
And a resting place for his searching soul.

People's Problems

Everyone has problems in this restless world of care,
Everyone grows weary with the crosses they must bear.
Everyone is troubled and their skies are overcast
As they try to face the future while still dwelling in the past.
But people with their problems only listen with one ear,
For people only listen to the things they want to hear,
And they only hear the things they are able to believe,
And the answers God gives they're not ready to receive.
So while the people's problems keep growing every day
And humans try to solve them in their own willful way,
God seeks to help and watches, waiting always patiently
To help them solve their problems, whatever they may be
So people of all nations may at last become aware
That God will solve their problems
Through faith and hope and prayer.

I will always have hope; I will praise you more and more.
Psalm 71:14 NIV

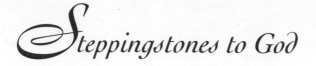 Steppingstones to God

An aching heart is but a steppingstone
To greater joy than you've ever known,
For things that cause the heart to ache
Until you think that it must break
Become the strength by which we climb
To higher heights that are sublime
And feel the radiance of God's smiles
When we have soared above life's trials.
So when you're overwhelmed with fears
And all your hopes are drenched in tears,
Think not that life has been unfair
And given you too much to bear,
For God has chosen you because,
With all your weaknesses and flaws,
He feels that you are worthy of
The greatness of His wondrous love.
So welcome every stumbling block
And every thorn and jagged rock,
For each one is a steppingstone
To God, who wants you for His own,

For discipline in daily duty
Will shape your life for deeper beauty,
And as you grow in strength and grace
The clearer you can see God's face,
And on the steppingstones of strife
You reach at last eternal life.

Take courage and be stouthearted, all you who hope in the LORD.
Psalm 31:25 NAB

The Way to God

He carried the cross to Calvary,
Carried its burdens for you and me,
There on the cross He was crucified,
And because He suffered and bled and died,
We know that whatever our cross may be,
It leads to God and eternity.
For who can hope for a crown of stars
Unless it is earned with suffering and scars,
For how could we face the living Lord
And rightfully claim His promised reward
If we have not carried our cross of care
And tasted the cup of bitter despair.
Let those who yearn for the pleasures of life
And long to escape all suffering and strife,
Rush recklessly on to an empty goal
With never a thought of the spirit and soul.
But if you are searching to find the way
To life everlasting and eternal day,
With faith in your heart, take the path He trod,
For the way of the cross is the way to God.

Under New Management

Nothing goes right—everything's wrong—
You stumble and fall as you trudge along.
The other guy wins and you always lose,
Whatever you hear is always bad news.
Well, here's some advice that's worth a try—
Businessmen use it when they want sales to soar high.
Old management goes and the new comes in,
For this is the way big business can win.
So if you are trying to manage your life,
Yet all around is chaos and strife,
Make up your mind that you too need a change
And start making plans to somehow rearrange
The way that you think and the things that you do
And whatever it is that is hindering you.
Then put yourself under God's management now,
And when He takes over you'll find that somehow
Everything changes—old things pass away
And the darkness of night becomes the brightness of day,
For God can transform and change into winners
The losers, the skeptics, and even the sinners.

Faith for Dark Days

When dark days come—and they come to us all—
We feel so helpless and lost and small.
We cannot fathom the reason why,
And it is futile for us to try
To find the answer, the reason or cause,
For the master plan is without any flaws,
And when the darkness shuts out the light,
We must lean on faith to restore our sight,
For there is nothing we need to know
If we have faith that wherever we go
God will be there to help us bear
Our disappointments, pain, and care,
For He is our Shepherd, our Father, our Guide,
And you're never alone with the Lord at your side.

All that I have seen teaches me to trust the Creator for all that I have not seen.

Ralph Waldo Emerson

The affection that
*   makes life worth living,*
*   bridges the here and now with eternity,*
*   improves life through acts of kindness done in a spirit of love —*
these are indeed aspects of hope.

Love is patient; love is kind. Love is not jealous, it does not put on airs, it is not snobbish. Love is never rude, it is not self seeking, it is not prone to anger; neither does it brood over injuries. Love does not rejoice in what is wrong but rejoices with the truth. There is no limit to love's forbearance, to its trust, its hope, its power to endure. Love never fails.

1 Corinthians 13:4–8 NAB

Love

People ask me the meaning of love. To me, true love is sharing and caring, giving and forgiving, loving and being loved, walking hand in hand, talking heart to heart, seeing through each other's eyes, laughing together, weeping together, praying together, and always trusting and believing and thanking God for each other. For love that is shared is a beautiful thing; it enriches the soul and makes the heart sing. What greater joy could there be than to share the love of God. Great is the power of might and mind, but only love can make us kind.

H.S.R.

Faith, Hope, and Love

Faith, hope, and love—more priceless than gold,
For if you possess them, you've riches untold,
For with faith to believe what your eyes cannot see
And hope to look forward to new joys to be
And love to transform the most commonplace
Into beauty and kindness and goodness and grace,
There's nothing too much to accomplish or do,
For with faith, hope, and love to carry you through,
Your life will be happy and full and complete,
For with faith, hope, and love, the bitter turns sweet—
For all earthly joys, and heaven's joys too,
Belong to God's children who are faithful and true.

There is hope for your future, says the LORD.
Jeremiah 31:17 RSV

Warm Our Hearts with Your Love

Oh, God who made the summer
   and warmed the earth with beauty,
Warm our hearts with gratitude
   and devotion to our duty,
For in this age of violence,
   rebellion and defiance,
We've forgotten the true meaning
   of dependable reliance.
We have lost our sense of duty
   and our sense of values too,
And what was once unsanctioned
   no longer is taboo.
Our standards have been lowered,
   and we resist all discipline,
And our vision has been narrowed
   and blinded to all sin.

Oh, put the summer brightness
   in our closed, unseeing eyes
So in the careworn faces
   that we pass we'll recognize
The heartbreak and the loneliness,
   the trouble and despair
That a word of understanding
   would make easier to bear.
Oh, God, look down on our cold hearts
   and warm them with Your love,
And grant us Your forgiveness,
   which we're so unworthy of.

*Hope is the . . . companion of power and the mother of success; for
whoso hopes strongly has within him the gift of miracles.*

Samuel Smiles

God Grant Us Hope, Faith, and Love

Hope for a world grown cynically cold,
Hungry for power and greedy for gold—
Faith to believe when, within and without,
There's a nameless fear in a world of doubt—
Love that is bigger than race or creed
To cover the world and fulfill each need . . .
God grant these gifts of faith, hope, and love—
Three things this world has so little of—
For only these gifts from our Father above
Can turn the world from hatred to love.

Of all the forces that make for a better world, none is so indispensable, none so powerful, as hope. Without hope men are only half alive. With hope they dream and think and work.

Charles Sawyer

Remember This

Great is the power of might and mind,
But only love can make us kind,
And all we are or hope to be
Is empty pride and vanity.
If love is not a part of all,
The greatest man is very small.

The command I give you is this, that you love one another.
John 15:17 NAB

The Power of Love

In this restless world of struggle
   it is often hard to find
Answers to the questions
   that disturb our peace of mind,
And our hearts are lost and lonely
   as we search to find the key
To the meaning of all living
   and to immortality.
But we'll never find the answers
   in science, graphs, and charts,
For the only real solution
   must be found within our hearts,
For the answer to all living
   God holds safely in His keeping,
And only when we know Him
   will we find what we are seeking—
For to know Him is to love Him,
   and to love Him is to find
The answer to all questions
   that fill every troubled mind.

*We look forward to the time when the Power of Love will replace
the Love of Power. Then will our world know the blessings of Peace.*
                                   William Ewart Gladstone

Folks Like You

It's folks like you we like to meet,
We like to see, we like to greet.
We like to talk and have them near
Because they bring good will and cheer
And leave a pleasant memory too
Whenever they are gone from you.
It's folks like you the whole world needs,
Who brighten living with hope-filled deeds.
It's folks like you, who lay no claim
To what the world accepts as fame,
Who are the folks who really rate
The honors of the truly great,
For what is greater than to be
Beloved by everyone you see?

*There are in the end three things that last: faith, hope, and love,
and the greatest of these is love.*

1 Corinthians 13:13 NAB

Lives Distressed Cannot Be Blessed

Refuse to be discouraged,
  refuse to be distressed,
For when we are despondent,
  our lives cannot be blessed—
For doubt and fear and worry
  close the door to faith and prayer,
And there's no room for blessings
  when we're lost in deep despair.
So remember when you're troubled
  with uncertainty and doubt,
It is best to tell our Father
  what our fear is all about—
For unless we seek His guidance
  when troubled times arise,
We are bound to make decisions
  that are twisted and unwise,
But when we view our problems
  through the eyes of God above,
Misfortunes turn to blessings
  and hatred turns to love.

The quality of
*   bearing annoyances without complaining,*
*   maintaining a calm and composed frame of mind,*
*   sustaining self-control in unpleasant circumstances —*
these are indeed aspects of hope.

Now hope that is seen is not hope. For who hopes for what he sees? But if we hope for what we do not see, we wait for it with patience.

Romans 8:24–25 RSV

Patience

These past few months I have been going through many hours of soul-searching and walking through dark hours that come to us all. But I know God is behind the dark cloud that engulfs me, and I must endure it until He moves the darkness, for this is not a destructive experience but a constructive one. I am sure He is trying to awaken me to a new awareness of how best to serve Him. And after my old self dies completely, I will have moved a little closer to God.

H.S.R.

My Daily Prayer

God, be my resting place
　and my protection
In hours of trouble,
　defeat, and dejection—
May I never give way
　to self-pity and sorrow,
May I always be sure
　of a better tomorrow,
May I stand undaunted,
　come what may,
Secure in the knowledge
　I have only to pray
And ask my Creator
　and Father above
To keep me serene
　in His grace and His love.

Rejoice in your hope, be patient in tribulation, be constant in prayer.
Romans 12:12 RSV

Blessings in Disguise

God sends His little angels in many forms and guises.
They come as lovely miracles that God alone devises.
He does nothing without purpose, everything's in a plan
To fulfill in bounteous measure all He ever promised man.
For every little angel with a body bent and broken
Or a mind quite challenged or with little words unspoken
Is just God's way of trying to reach out and touch the hand
Of all who do not know Him and cannot understand
That often through an angel whose wings will never fly
The Lord is pointing out the way to His eternal sky,
Where there will be no handicaps of body, soul, or mind
And where all limitations will be dropped and left behind.
So accept these little angels as gifts from God above,
And thank Him for this lesson in faith and hope and love.

Love Divine,
All Loves Excelling

In a myriad of miraculous ways
God shapes our lives and changes our days.
Beyond our will or even knowing
God keeps our spirits ever growing—
For lights and shadows, sun and rain,
Sadness and gladness, joy and pain
Combine to make our lives complete
And give us victory through defeat.
Oh, "Love divine, all loves excelling"
In troubled hearts You just keep dwelling,
Patiently waiting for a prodigal son
To say at last, "Thy will be done."

*The person who has a firm trust in the Supreme Being is powerful
in his power, wise by his wisdom, happy by his happiness.*

Joseph Addison

Daily Prayers
Dissolve Your Cares

I meet God in the morning
    and go with Him through the day,
Then in the stillness of the night
    before sleep comes I pray
That God will just take over
    all the problems I couldn't solve,
And in the peacefulness of sleep
    my cares will all dissolve,
So when I open up my eyes
    to greet another day,
I'll find myself renewed in strength
    and there will open up a way
To meet what seemed impossible
    for me to solve alone,
And once again I'll be assured
    I am never on my own.

For if we try to stand alone,
   we are weak and we will fall,
For God is always greatest
   when we're helpless, lost, and small,
But no day is unmeetable
   if, on rising, our first thought
Is to thank God for the blessings
   that His loving care has brought—
For there can be no failures
   or hopeless, unsaved sinners
If we enlist the help of God,
   who makes all losers winners.
So meet Him in the morning
   and go with Him through the day,
And thank Him for His guidance
   each evening when you pray,
And if you follow faithfully
   this daily way to pray,
You will never in your lifetime
   face another hopeless day.

I rise before dawn and cry for help; I have put my hope in your word.
Psalm 119:147 NIV

Faith Is a Mighty Fortress

Instead of hearts filled with joy and cheer,
We've mixed emotions of hope and fear —
Hope for the peace we long have sought,
Fear that our hopes will come to naught.
Unwilling to trust in the Father's will,
We count on our logic and shallow skill,
And in our arrogance and pride,
We are no longer satisfied
To place our confidence and love
With childlike faith in God above,
For faith in things we cannot see
Requires a child's simplicity.
Faith alone can save man's soul
And lead him to a higher goal,
For there's but one unfailing course —
We win by faith and not by force.

*Let us hold unswervingly to the hope we profess, for he who
promised is faithful.*

Hebrews 10:23 NIV

Hope for Every Day

God, grant me courage and hope for every day,
Faith to guide me along my way,
Understanding and patience too,
And grace to accept what life gives me to do.

Give Me the Contentment of Acceptance

In the deep, dark hours of my distress,
My unworthy life seems a miserable mess.
Handicapped, limited, with my strength decreasing,
The demands on my time keep forever increasing,
And I pray for the flair and the force of youth
So I can keep spreading God's light and His truth,
For my heart's happy hope and my dearest desire
Is to continue to serve You with fervor and fire,
But I no longer have strength to dramatically do
The spectacular things I loved doing for You,
Forgetting entirely that all You required
Was not a servant the world admired
But a humbled heart and a sanctified soul
Whose only mission and purpose and goal

Was to be content with whatever God sends
And to know that to please You really depends
Not on continued and mounting success
But on learning how to become less and less
And to realize that we serve God best
When our one desire and only request
Is not to succumb to worldly acclaim
But to honor ourselves in Your holy name.

Behold, the eye of the LORD is on those who fear him, on those who hope in his steadfast love.

Psalm 33:18 RSV

This Is Just a Resting Place

Sometimes the road of life seems long
    as we travel through the years,
And with hearts that are broken
    and eyes brimful of tears,
We falter in our weariness
    and sink beside the way,
But God leans down and whispers,
    "Child, there'll be another day."
And the road will grow much smoother
    and much easier to face,
So do not be disheartened—
    this is just a resting place.

When our hopes break, let our patience hold.
Thomas Fuller

Sleepy Hollow

Nestled by the river,
　sheltered by the trees
Rests a little haven—
　one of nature's symphonies.
In this tranquil rendezvous
　where peace and beauty blend,
There is a sweet communion
　in the meeting of a friend,
For in this shining solitude
　false values slip away,
And only truth and beauty
　seem planted there to stay.
In this refreshing refuge
　all doors are opened wide
So faith and hope and happiness
　can always step inside.
They call it Sleepy Hollow,
　but the name I like the best
Is just the house of happiness
　where weary travelers rest.

Faith is confident assurance concerning what we hope for, and conviction about things we do not see.

Hebrews 11:1 NAB

God Help Us Again

O God, our help in ages past,
   our hope in years to be,
Look down upon the present
   and see our need of Thee.
For in this age of unrest,
   with danger all around,
We need Thy hand to lead us
   to a higher, safer ground.
We need Thy help and counsel
   to make us more aware
That our safety and security
   lie solely in Thy care.
Give us strength and courage
   to be honorable and true,
Practicing Thy precepts
   in everything we do.
And keep us ever humble
   in the greatness of Thy love
So someday we are fit to dwell
   with Thee in peace above.

Have courage for the great sorrows of life and patience for the small ones; and when you have laboriously accomplished your daily task, go to sleep in peace. God is awake.

Victor Hugo

A Prayer for Patience

God, teach me to be patient,
   teach me to go slow,
Teach me how to wait on You
   when my way I do not know.
Teach me sweet forbearance
   when things do not go right
So I remain unruffled
   when others grow uptight.
Teach me how to quiet
   my racing, rising heart
So I might hear the answer
   You are trying to impart.
Teach me to let go, dear God,
   and pray undisturbed until
My heart is filled with inner peace
   and I learn to know Your will.

The attribute that
    permits the placement of confidence in a source other than self,
    generates dependability, integrity, and responsibility,
    denotes credence and properly placed reliance —
these are indeed aspects of hope.

The world answers back to our faith. It trusts when we trust. It responds to our confidence.

Hugh Thompson Kerr

rust

I just know everything that has ever happened in my life, whether it was good or bad, glad or sad, God sent it for a reason, and I truly believe with all my heart that God never makes mistakes. I never question what God sends, for I realize, when you question God, you lose the unquestionable power of trust and you no longer can enjoy its endless benefits. There is nothing I need know or even try to understand if I place myself completely in God's great and mighty hand.

H.S.R.

There's Always a Springtime

After the winter comes the spring
To show us that in everything
There's always renewal divinely planned—
Flawlessly perfect, the work of God's hand.
And just like the seasons that come and go,
When the flowers of spring lie buried in snow,
God sends to the heart in its winter of sadness
A springtime awakening of new hope and gladness,
And loved ones who sleep in a season of death
Will too be awakened by God's life-giving breath.

If seeds in the black earth can turn into such beautiful roses, what might not the heart of man become in its long journey toward the stars?

Gilbert Keith Chesterton

A Child's Prayer

Hear me, blessed Jesus,
   as I say my prayers today
And tell me You are close to me
   and You'll never go away.
Tell me that You love me
   like the Bible says You do,
And tell me also, Jesus,
   I can always come to You
And You will understand me
   when other people don't,
And though some may forget me,
   just tell me that You won't.
Jesus, stay real close to me
   at home and school and play,
For I will feel much braver
   if You're never far away.
And sometimes when I'm naughty,
   I hope You won't be sad,
For really I don't mean to do
   anything that's bad.

Most of all, dear Jesus,
   I want to tell you that I know
Our Father sent You to us
   to live on earth below
So little children like myself
   would know You too were small
And that You are our dearest Friend
   and that You understand us all.
And some day when I'm older
   I will show you it is true
That even as a little child,
   my heart belonged to you.

We had from childhood not only the experience of love and truth common to all family life, but the idea of them embodied in the person of Jesus, a picture always present to our imagination as well as our feelings.

Joyce Cary

Thy Will Be Done

God did not promise sun without rain,
Light without darkness or joy without pain.
He only promised strength for the day
When the darkness comes and we lose our way.
For only through sorrow do we grow more aware
That God is our refuge in times of despair,
For when we are happy and life's bright and fair,
We often forget to kneel down in prayer.
But God seems much closer and needed much more
When trouble and sorrow stand outside our door,
For then we seek shelter in His wondrous love,
And we ask Him to send us help from above.
And that is the reason we know it is true
That bright, shining hours and dark, sad ones too
Are part of the plan God made for each one,
And all we can pray is "Thy will be done."
So know that you are never alone
For God is your Father and you're one of His own.

He Is Always There

In sickness or health,
In suffering and pain,
In storm-laden skies,
In sunshine and rain,
God always is there
To lighten your way
And lead you through darkness
To a much brighter day.

You are my refuge and my shield; I have put my hope in your word.
Psalm 119:114 NIV

God's Promises Prevail

In this uncertain world of trouble
   with its sorrow, sin, and strife,
Man needs a haven for his heart
   to endure the storms of life.
He keeps hoping for a promise
   of better, bigger things
With the power and the prestige
   that fame and fortune bring.
The world is rife with promises
   that are fast and falsely spoken,
For man in his deceptive way
   knows his promise can be broken.
But when God makes a promise,
   it remains forever true,
For everything God promises
   He unalterably will do.